Book of Lyrics

Book of Lyrics

by WITTER BYNNER

Alfred A Knopf 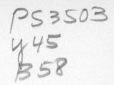 1958
New York

Library of Congress Catalog Card Number 55-9274

© Witter Bynner, 1955

This is a Borzoi Book

PUBLISHED BY ALFRED A. KNOPF, INC.

Published November 14, 1955
Second printing, April 1958

for

MIRANDA MASOCCO

Note

Twenty years having passed since publication of *Selected Poems*, I here reprint a second time from books issued before then—*Grenstone Poems*, *The Beloved Stranger*, *A Canticle of Pan*, *Caravan*, and *Indian Earth*—and add from two later volumes—*Against the Cold* and *Take Away the Darkness*—such verse in lyric mood as I continue to like best.

For permission to use a considerable number of still later lyrics, which have until now not appeared in book-form, I thank the editors of *The Dallas Times Herald*, *The Freeman*, *Gentry*, *The Lyric*, *The New Mexico Quarterly*, *The New Yorker*, *The Saturday Review*, and *The University of Kansas City Review*.

Readers might well miss in these pages the presence of Laotzu, the T'ang poets, Euripides or Charles Vildrac; but I have decided to omit any of my English versions of Chinese, Greek or French originals as being only verbally mine.

Though inclusion of poems as pondered as *Gothic* and *A Shepherd of Stars* might be questioned, or as long as *Epithalamium and Elegy*, *A Dance for Rain*, and *Passing Near*, I have put aside doubt in the belief that the poem's nature or cadence so warranted. And I have disjoined from two poems each published as a book—*The New World* and *Eden Tree*—several passages which I feel to be in themselves lyrically complete.

W. B.

Contents

Summer

Autumn

Winter

Epilogue

Prologue

The Wind at the Candle

Age has its merriment as well as youth,
   And both of them go flying
And either time, to tell the truth,
   Is a likely time for dying.

Be your own ancestor when callow,
   Be your own son when sere—
For wicks, when wind is at the tallow,
   Bend and veer.

Spring

A Stream

Cool, moving, fruitful and alive I go,
In my small run reflecting all the sky.
I see through trees, I see through melting snow,
I see through riffles which the wind and I
Have made, and through the shadow of a man,
Nor know where I arrive, where I began.

Spring at the Door

Spring is a wild thing for sure—
    What wilder ever ran?
But once in a while he will rub at the door
    Of almost any man,
And here he is at my own sill,
    Whining for me to know,
Until I peer outside and feel
    A flurry in the snow,
Find a cloud of shining flakes,
    A blur of foot-prints four,
From a wild thing that comes and shakes
    The quiet of my door.

Garden

See me crouching,
    Part of a tree,
You look on a garden,
    Looking on me.

These roots commingle
    From their birth,
And so do I
    With all the earth.

Songs

I have an impulse every day
    But it would never do:
I want to walk a different way,
    Reversing shoe and shoe.

I want my left foot to go right,
    My right foot to go wrong.
The impulse quickens every night,
    And that is half my song.

At night I wear no shoes at all,
    My feet go as they will,
One of them walking up a wall,
    The other on a sill.

The windowed foot is out and in,
    The walled foot in and out.
Songs never end, only begin,
    And what are they about?

Spring Tendril

Such an incessant tendril!—
The quiet crashing of a tendril
Upward from earth into the air!

I sat and watched for a long time.
It was incessant there,
Unfolding minutely with brasses
Of symphony up through the grasses
Into air
And with woodwinds and with human voices
And with the incessant care that rejoices
And with small leaves which fare
Forth into air and which dare
To be bare and to share
Bareness and boldness and wonder with other leaves
Of wonder until nothing is left which bereaves.

One vein while I watched awoke
And crept toward heaven.
Three veins awoke
And then eleven.

All spring came alive, though nothing moved
Save one small living tendril which I loved.

Prodigal Son

What was given
   Me by birth
Was not heaven,
   It was earth.

Though some other
   House be fine,
Strange old father,
   This is mine.

To No One in Particular

Locate your love, you lose your love,
   Find her, you look away . . .
Though mine I never quite discern,
   I trace her every day.

She has a thousand presences,
   As surely seen and heard
As birds that hide behind a leaf
   Or leaves that hide a bird.

Single your love, you lose your love,
   You cloak her face with clay;
Now mine I never quite discern—
   And never look away.

Iris

By the faint beard of the iris
I am very young tonight,
I am wicked and desirous
   Of delight.

I who guarded many a garden,
I who watered every want,
Would no longer be the warden
   Of a plant.

I would lose my sense entirely
And go wanton in a wood
And would treat a petal direly
   If I could.

For it's so that spring can fire us
With the lunacy we feared
And can make us pluck an iris
   By the beard.

The Wild Star

There is a star whose bite is certain death
   While the moon but makes you mad—
So run from stars till you are out of breath
   On a spring night, my lad,
Or slip among the shadows of a pine
   And hide face down from the sky
And never stir and never make a sign
   Till the wild star goes by.

Love-Song

Plough me under with new wonder,
   Grow me with listening ears,
Top and tassel me asunder,
   Freshen me with tears.

Pledge me with silk upon my lips
   From scented windrift hair
And set upon my fingertips
   Your fingers kernel-bare.

Place all your ribs against my own
   In furrows of delight
And there shall be new harvest grown
   Under the moon at night.

A Wild Thing

Your will was lighter than a wing,
   You were purposeless with song.
And so I asked you not to sing
   But only to belong—
And so I asked you not to be
   The wild thing I love.
What in the world was the matter with me?
   What was I thinking of?

When the First Bird Sang

I loved you, loved you, with your unseen eyes
Sweet to my lips in nearnesses of night,
Sweet to my fingers that were trembling light
Upon your face to prove my true surmise
Of eyes that opened, witnessing with mine.
There had been no sign at all nor ray of sight,
But only love to prompt my guess aright . . .
Then dawn revealed you slowly line by line.

At first I held away your dreaming face
From my face. Till the dark blue light was keen,
Still, still I held it—though my passion beat
For it. And then all heaven on that place
Came down, since nothing ever to be seen
Again could hide your eyes, so wild, so sweet!

Lament

There is a chill deeper than that of death,
In the return of the beloved and not of love.
And there is no warmth for it
But the warmth of a world which needs more than the sun,
Or the warmth of lament for beauty
Which is graven on many stones.

Someone was there . . .
I put out my hand in the dark
And felt
The long fingers of the wind.
And yet I would be with you a little while,
Dear ghost.

The Patient to the Doctors

Name me no name for my disease,
   With uninforming breath;
I tell you I am none of these,
   But homesick unto death—

Homesick for hills that I had known,
   For brooks that I had crossed,
Before I met this flesh and bone
   And followed and was lost . . .

Save that they broke my heart at last,
   Name me no name of ills.
Say only, 'Here is where he passed,
   Seeking again those hills.'

Squanderings

Be aware
That goods are brittle,
That those who have little often break that little
While those who have much take care.

Love is not a wealth to scatter,
To forsake.
Loneliness is hard to break.
Squanderings matter.

To a Light-Hearted Friend

You are of air, my boy,
No earth connects with you,
No arrow yet has pierced your joy
For pain to enter through.

And lightly I commend
Your free and easy wing,
Also its element, my friend.
Earth is a heavy thing.

A Long Lean Fellow

A long lean fellow lives nearby
   Whom I like as well as most,
But there's a distance in his eye
   As vacant as a ghost.

He waves his hand in the morning light,
   I wave mine back to him,
And then his figure, which was bright,
   Grows dim.

And though I clearly hear repeat
   The sound of his footfall,
There's only, moving down the street,
   A shadow on a wall.

Spring and a Mother Dead

I who should write her epitaph
   Would err:
What could I say to anyone
   But her?

Apricot-blossoms open
   Like a bell:
But this time there is nobody
   To tell.

The Two Windows

Out of my western window,
The purple clouds are dying
Edged with fire;
And out of my eastern window,
The full round moon is rising
Formed of ice.

So beautiful,
Although the day go by
And the night come on forever,
Is this momentary world.

The Kite

Moments when sap stirs in the trees and when
Hard buds with springtime melt
Have brought alive in me again
Sap which my boyhood felt
When my young hands took up a string to play
Direction on its own unhurtful way.

The Sowers

Now horses' hooves are treading earth again
To start the wheat from darkness into day,
And along the heavy field go seven men
With hands on ploughs and eyes on furrowing clay.

Six of the men are old; but one, a boy,
Knows in his heart that more than fields are sown—
For spring is ploughing heaven with rows of joy
In the voice of one high bird, singing alone.

Child

The child knows well,
Might even tell
If elders would but listen,
What makes the sheen
Upon a bean
Like the whole world glisten,
Knows that the sky
Is not too high
And finds his finger telling
Just what it is
That manages
The ocean in its swelling.

I Need No Sky

I need no sky nor stars
When once, beyond the bars
That fence a meadow in,
I have espied a place
Blowing with Queen Anne's lace
Where only stones had been.

New stars have come my way,
Encompassing by day
A constellation's rim;
And, if I dared before
To doubt, I doubt no more
But do believe in Him,

This Hermit who, unknown
To eye or ear, has sown
In a secretive hour,
This Stranger who can make
The whole of heaven wake
And wander in a flower.

Summer

A Wanderer

As when a bird alights at sea,
I found you and you rested me.

But soon again I wandered free—
For so a sea-bird loves the sea.

The Enchanted Swans

Out of a fairy-tale they flew above me,
Three white wild swans with silk among their wings—
And one might be a princess and might love me,
If I had not forgotten all such things.

They flew abreast and would not pause nor quicken,
One of them guarded by the other two,
And left me helpless here, alone and stricken,
Without the secret that I thought I knew.

Cockcrow

O come, announcer, tell me once again
That the sun arises, that the moon will wane
And yet still wax, soothe me against the shock
In veins less lasting than a vein of rock.

Ancestral world, face me, I face you.
This is your bounden duty and mine too.
Open that great dumb mouth and speak at last
The secret which we both have held too fast.

Eyes, eyes, I see you, raindrops glancing by,
Stars in the far, unconscionable sky
And people, people, most of them in love.
What is this death that we are thinking of?

Give me the clasp that everybody wants
But not the clutch too close that ever haunts
Each one of us and leaves us with a stare
Into our ancestry and into air.

Loosen Your Marrow

That little tangled thing you call your brain,
Which has not lived before nor will again
In any such compartment of distress,
Is an abominable restlessness.

Loosen your marrow from corrupting thought
And be as inattentive as you ought
To all the little motions of the will
That feed upon the happiness they kill.

Open your being to the flows of air
That form its destiny from everywhere—
And let your mind become a native feather
And not a nest of worms, tangled together.

Grass-Tops

What bird are you in the grass-tops?
Your poise is enough of an answer,
With your wing-tips like up-curving fingers
Of the slow-moving hands of a dancer . . .

And what is so nameless as wonder,
Which poets, who give it a name,
Are only unnaming forever?—
Content, though it go, that it came.

A Beautiful Mexican

There where she sips her wine, her copper brow
Is itself the sunset. Now she has lifted her eyes,
And they are evening stars. I have seen many
Mexican sunsets—but never before had I seen one
Come down from the mountain to be a beautiful woman,
To shadow a table with a dusk of light
From a bare arm and then, alas, to rise
And turn and go, leaving a sudden darkness.

A Dance for Rain

You may never see rain, unless you see
A dance for rain at Cochiti,
Never hear thunder in the air
Unless you hear the thunder there,
Nor know the lightning in the sky
If there's no pole to know it by.
They dipped the pole just as I came,
And I can never be the same
Since those feathers gave my brow
The touch of wind that's on it now,
Bringing over the arid lands
Butterfly gestures from Hopi hands
And holding me, till earth shall fail,
As close to earth as a fox's tail.

I saw them, naked, dance in line
Before the candles of a leafy shrine:
Before a saint in a Christian dress
I saw them dance their holiness,
I saw them reminding him all day long
That death is weak and life is strong
And urging the fertile earth to yield
Seed from the loin and seed from the field.

A feather in the hair and a shell at the throat
Were lifting and falling with every note

Of the chorus-voices and the drum,
Calling for the rain to come.
A fox on the back, and shaken on the thigh
Rain-cloth woven from the sky,
And under the knee a turtle-rattle
Clacking with the toes of sheep and cattle—
These were the men, their bodies painted
Earthen, with a white rain slanted;
These were the men, a windy line,
Their elbows green with a growth of pine.
And in among them, close and slow,
Women moved, the way things grow,
With a mesa-tablet on the head
And a little grassy creeping tread
And with sprays of pine moved back and forth,
While the dance of the men blew from the north,
Blew from the south and east and west
Over the field and over the breast.
And the heart was beating in the drum,
Beating for the rain to come.
   Dead men out of earlier lives,
Leaving their graves, leaving their wives,
Were partly flesh and partly clay,
And their heads were corn that was dry and gray.

They were ghosts of men and once again
They were dancing like a ghost of rain;
For the spirits of men, the more they eat,
Have happier hands and lighter feet,
And the better they dance the better they know
How to make corn and children grow.
   And so in Cochiti that day,
They slowly put the sun away
And they made a cloud and they made it break
And they made it rain for the children's sake.
And they never stopped the song or the drum
Pounding for the rain to come.
   The rain made many suns to shine,
Golden bodies in a line
With leaping feather and swaying pine.
And the brighter the bodies, the brighter the rain
Where thunder heaped it on the plain.
Arroyos had been empty, dry,
But now were running with the sky;
And the dancers' feet were in a lake,
Dancing for the people's sake.
And the hands of a ghost became a cup
For scooping handfuls of water up;

And he poured it into a ghostly throat,
And he leaped and waved with every note
Of the dancers' feet and the songs of the drum
That had called the rain and made it come.
　For this was not a god of wood,
This was a god whose touch was good,
You could lie down in him and roll
And wet your body and wet your soul;
For this was not a god in a book,
This was a god whom you tasted and took
Into a cup that you made with your hands,
Into your children and into your lands—
This was a god that you could see,
Rain, rain, in Cochiti!

Three Friends

Beside a ditch bringing water
To corn not yet tall
Three men were sitting with poems on their knees,
And they heard the wind rise and fall,
And one of them heard his own voice rising,
And one of them heard his own voice falling,
And the other heard only the summons of the wind
And wondered where it was calling.

A Thrush in the Moonlight

In came the moon and covered me with wonder,
Touched me and was near me and made me very still.
In came a rush of song, like rain after thunder,
Pouring importunate on my window-sill.

I lowered my head, I hid it, I would not see nor hear,
The birdsong had stricken me, had brought the moon too near.
But when I dared to lift my head, night began to fill
With singing in the darkness. And then the thrush grew still.
And the moon came in, and silence, on my window-sill.

Out of the Sea

With your sun-white hair and your smile
And your body as white as a white sea-bird,
I took you and held you and watched you awhile
   And never a word.

Nothing to say, to explain
Or to answer, nothing to hear or be heard,
Only to kiss you again and again
   With never a word.

Even lately I cannot be sure.
It seems in my sleep that we neither have stirred,
So silent you vanished, so sweet you endure,
   And never a word.

Moving Leaves

How could I know the wisdom of a world
That blows its withered leaves down from the air
They gleamed in once and gathers their strength again upward
In the sap of earth, if I set my fervid heart
On a leaf unmoved by any wind of change,
If I wanted still that spring when first I loved?
No leaves that have ever fallen anywhere
Are anywhere but here, heaping the trees.

Celia

From the lane I turn to look,
   Till my eyes are cool with seeing:
Bright before me comes a brook
   Out of branches into being.

And behind me, while I turn,
   Follows the familiar pace . . .
Till, at last, I look and learn—
   Seeing Celia face to face.

Out of whispers of concealment
   Like the brook my Celia slips,
Bringing me the dear revealment—
   For I ask her, and her lips

Tell me that where leaves were green
   Close beside her often moved
Someone she had never seen,
   Someone she had always loved.

Time

I do not know what year it is,
  I do not what day,
The reason being clear, it is
    That you have gone away.

And yet this is the way it is,
  I shall not know what year
Or hour of the day it is
    When you are surely here.

Calendar

Why should I know or care what month it is?
An Aztec calendar was made long since.
What year was it? What century? What matter?
A piece of stone becomes symmetrical.
If I watch the time, some of my friends will die,
If I watch the time, I shall surely die myself.
Let me, then, gather all my friends about me
And carve an endless moment out of stone.

Voices

Oh, there were lights and laughter
   And the motions to and fro
Of people as they enter
   And people as they go
And there were many voices
   Vying at the feast,
But mostly I remember
   Yours who spoke the least.

Sky-Change

Sky-changes come and go
And breathlessness
Goes with them: a friend's
Death is too difficult to know;
A bird's flight ends.
But you are here no less.
You are all these things
That shift and dart,
Breaking the heart
With life stranger than death.
You catch my breath
Away from me, you make the air
Almost too sweet to bear
With sky-change and wings.

Laurel

I will not call you beautiful again,
Though my throat ache with the silence of refraining,
And not a sigh will I explain,
Though my hands fill with explaining.

For you are as beautiful as a hill I know
In spring, breathing with light—
But as soon as I told you, a chill like snow
Covered and turned you white.

I will not call you beautiful again,
Your labyrinthine loveliness I will not name.
I will be silent as forgotten men
Dead beyond blame.

No matter how your airs of spring beguile,
Be it my fortitude, my courage, my endeavor,
Not to acclaim the laurel of your smile—
Except today, to-morrow and forever!

Haven

Seeing your face,
I am sheltered by a place
Of unaccountably expected grace
From cold and snow,
Yet do not surely know
Whether the haven is now or long ago.

Lightning

There is a solitude in seeing you,
Followed by your presence when you are gone.
You are like heaven's veins of lightning.
I cannot see till afterward
How beautiful you are.
There is a blindness in seeing you,
Followed by the sight of you when you are gone.

Dream

I had returned from dreaming—
When there came the look of you
And I could not tell after that,
And the sound of you
And I could not tell,
And at last the touch of you
And I could tell then less than ever,
Though I silvered and fell
As at the very mountain-brim
Of dream.

For how could the motion of a shadow in a field
Be a person?
Or the flash of an oriole-wing
Be a smile?
Or the turn of a leaf on a stream
Be a hand?
Or a bright breath of sun
Be lips?

I can reach out and out—and nothing will be there . . .
None of these things are true.
All of them are dreams—
There are neither streams
Nor leaves nor orioles nor you.

Lotuses

Deliver me, O beloved, from this evil
Of possessing you too near my hungry side
Or my hands or my lips, undo my passionate purpose
Of knowing you, become again as wide
As the night is, be wonderful with unknown stars
Far from the rim of touch, and hold so deep
A quietness that down the dim lake of heaven
We float away on lotuses of sleep.

Shadows

When the moonlight brings to my bed a fragrance of
   apple blossoms,
Why do I dream of frost among their petals?
Why do I dream of winter covering with snow
Even their shadows on my window-sill?

The Wave

You come with the light on your face
Of the turn of a river from trees to the open sun,
You are the wandering spirit of the most beloved place—
And yet you are a joy not there begun
Nor anywhere, but always about to be,
The invisible succeeding crest
That follows from the open sea
And shall be loveliest.

I have no language, hardly any word
To name you with, I have no flight of hands
To swim your surface closer than a bird:
For endless changing countermands
Your face and blinds me blacker than a crest of sun,
O joy not yet begun
But only about to be,
O sweet invisible unceasing wave
Following me, following me,
Through the sea-like grave!

A Tent Song

Till we watch the last low star,
Let us love and let us take
Of each other all we are.

On some morning with that star
One of us shall lie awake,
Lonely for the other's sake.

Breath

When so I lean my hand upon your shoulder,
When so I let my fingers fall forward
To the delicate arch of the breath,
To this most palpable cover and mold
Of the waves of life,
It is not you nor love I love—but life itself.

I look at you with a stranger, older intimacy,
I forget who you are whom I love,
With your temporal face,
I forget this or any of the generations
And its temporal face
And the lovely curious fallacy of choice.

Beyond the incomprehensible madness
Of the shoulder and the breast,
Above the tumult of obliteration,
I sow and reap upon the clouded tops of mountains
And am myself both sown and harvested,
And, from afar off, I behold, forget, achieve
You and myself and all things,
When so I let my hand fall forward
To the remote circumference of breath.

Encounter

Yours is a presence lovelier than death,
Heavy with blossoms, poignant of the sea.
The dead are magical but O, your breath
Has given more than lordly death to me.
I am your lover and a cloud is my crest,
The headland is my chariot, my waves go four abreast.

Let me be fleet and sunlit in your sight
A little while, before I charge and drown . . .
Then, O my love, who have so lavished might
On me that I would strike mortality down,
When in the end I fall, trampled by the sea,
Slain by my horses, I shall know your blossoms blinding me.

The Boatmen

A nearing benison of boatmen singing . . .
Can they be bringing to me a new wonder?

They are waiting in the night, as for a passenger . . .
But who would embark now with no light at all?

The dark is shaking like a tambourine . . .
They are taking my old wonder.

Earth

Desperate our pressure is
Of union and of kiss to kiss:
But we are made of mortal stuff:
Earth will bed us close enough.

At the Last

There is no denying
That it matters little,
When through a narrow door
We enter a room together,
Which goes after, which before.

Perhaps you are not dying:
Perhaps—there is no knowing—
I shall slip by and turn and laugh with you
Because it mattered so little,
The order of our going.

Stillness

You might suddenly be as far
As light upon an unseen star,
   So still you are.

Not now a wave for seas to fill
You might be stone on any hill,
   You are so still.

Epitaph

She who could not bear dispute
Nor unquiet now is mute,
She who could leave unsaid
Perfect silence now is dead.

During a Chorale by Cesar Franck

In an old chamber softly lit
  We heard the Chorale played,
And where you sat, an exquisite
Image of life and lover of it,
  Death sang a serenade.

I know now, Celia, what you heard
  And why you turned and smiled.
It was the white wings of a bird
Offering flight, and you were stirred
  Like an adventurous child.

Death sang, 'O lie upon your bier,
  Uplift your countenance!'
Death bade me be your cavalier,
Called me to march and shed no tear
  But sing to you and dance.

And when you followed, lured and led
  By those mysterious wings,
And when I knew that you were dead,
I could not weep. I sang instead
  As a true lover sings.

Passing Near

I had not till to-day been sure,
  But now I know:
Dead men and women come and go
  Under the pure
  Sequestering snow.

And under the autumnal fern
  And carmine bush,
Under the shadow of a thrush,
  They move and learn;
  And in the rush

Of all the mountain-brooks that wake
  With upward fling,
To brush and break the loosening cling
  Of ice, they shake
  The air with spring.

I had not till to-day been sure,
  But now I know:
Dead youths and maidens come and go
  Beneath the lure
  And undertow

Of cities, under every street
  Of empty stress,
Or heart of an adulteress—
  Each loud retreat
  Of lovelessness.

For only by the stir we make
  In passing near
Are we confused and cannot hear
  The ways they take
  Certain and clear.

Today I happened in a place
  Where all around
Was silence; until, underground,
  I heard a pace,
  A happy sound—

And people there, whom I could see,
  Tenderly smiled,
While under a wood of silent wild
  Antiquity
  Wandered a child,

Leading his mother by the hand,
　Happy and slow,
Teaching his mother where to go
　Under the snow . . .
Not even now I understand.
　I only know.

Autumn

A Shepherd of Stars

Stars are my sheep. Nobody clips
　　Gain of my shepherding.
The air comes cool upon my lips
　　Like water from a spring,
And out I stretch my finger-tips
　　And count my flock and sing:

'Come, graze beside me on my hill,
　　You little starry sheep—
Gather and eat your silver fill
　　And call me out of sleep
To trace you by your silver trill,
　　To fold you in my keep.'

Except myself, nobody cares
　　How many I shall bring—
Save Celia. And no other dares
　　To steal them while I sing . . .
Yet toward a world of common wares
　　The wind is beckoning:

'O, come and leave your silly sheep
   That wander up and down,
That cannot even earn their keep,
   O, come to town, to town!
A countryman is counted cheap,
   A shepherd is a clown!'

Stars are my sheep. Nobody knows
   How often in the fold
I enter with them when it snows
   And cannot feel the cold—
And yet it seems a wise man goes
   Where wool and meat are sold.

'O starry sheep, good-bye, good-bye—
   Your shepherd goes to town!
But never one of you shall die
   To clothe and feed the clown—
For you shall keep my hill, while I
   Shall wander up and down.'

A Letter

When I walked home forgotten,
When I walked home in grief,
I found a letter under my door.
It was an autumn leaf.

Solitude

No cave may be so deep
As the one that a hermit chooses to enter,
Not even sleep;
But if it has cracks in it from the very center,
Down he may go and close his eyes to tears
As Buddha sat,
But water drips in about his ears
And the dark stirs with a bat.

To a Young Inquirer

It is better sometimes that there be no f
Only a mist of blossom blown away:
If never flower had ripened from the root
Long since, it would be Eden still, they say.

Yet if the tempering and seasoning
May come to you as they have come to me,
I wish for you the broken breath of spring
And the salt of wintry cypress by the sea.

Watch how a petal drifts upon your hand
And pales and withers. Watch another passing,
Light in the air. Watch how the waters stand
And fall along the shore, ebbing and massing.

Let only fools fathom the more or less
Of melancholy and of happiness.

Withheld Warning

When I see another youth
Trying to discover truth,
Trying to disprove his follies,
Lying with a love for solace,
Why do I withhold a warning
That his heart is old by morning?
Much though we have cared to mingle,
Pain is paired and joy single.

The Singing Huntsman

The huntswoman-moon was my mother
  And the song-man, Apollo, my sire;
And I know either trick like the other,
  The trick of the bow and the lyre.

When beauty darts by me or lingers,
  When it folds or opens its wing,
On bow and on lyre are my fingers,
  And I shoot, and I sing.

The Dead Loon

There is a dead loon in the camp tonight, killed by a clever fool,
And down the lake a live loon calling.
The wind comes stealing, tall, muscular and cool,
From his plunge where stars are falling—
The wind comes creeping, stalking,
On his night-hidden trail,
Up to the cabin where we sit playing cards and talking.
And only I, of them all, listen and grow pale.
He glues his face to the window, addressing only me,
Talks to me of death and bids me hark
To the hollow scream of a loon and bids me see
The face of a clever fool reflected in the dark.

That dead loon is farther on the way than we are.
It has no voice, where it hangs nailed to the gate.
But it is with me now and with the evening star.
Its voice is my voice and its fate my fate.

An Old Elegy for a Child

O earth, with flowers on his eyes
  Be thou as sweet as he—
Be thou as light where now he lies
  As he was light on thee.

A Country Cottage

Than this there is no wiser funeral:
To choose a box with windows and with doors
Planted above the ground and to forestall
The peace of death, aware of it as yours.

You set your garden with calendulas;
Flesh of your flesh, they bear you to the sun,
And all the multitudinous life that was
Is quiet in this death you have begun.

It takes so little room to lie in peace,
So little motion to contain content,
There comes so little change with your decease,
So little difference to the firmament.

This Reed

What is this reed that grows tall in the river-bed?
They make their plaited mats of it to lie on,
They gather it from the river-beds and make mats of it
And soften their earthen floors with it to lie on . . .
Yesterday noon I saw the mat I needed,
Six feet of reeds torn loose from the river-bed,
A mat—which I might peacefully have lain on—
Go blowing down the lake before the wind.

Sands

I lay on a dune and slept,
Sharp grasses by my head:
While armies far-off warred and wept,
I joined the earth instead . . .
Until I moved my hand
And was awake again
And shook myself out of the sand
To the cold wind of men.

Prayer

Let us not look upon
Their like again,
This generation
Of bewildered men—
With earth-roads, sea-roads,
Sky-roads too, that show
All ways to enter
And no way to go.

Sunset

I will not look at the sun tonight,
   I have looked at it before.
I have seen suffusing in its light
   The end of human lore.

The very last of Troy went down
   And the very last of Rome—
And the very last of London Town
   And the very last of home.

Lot's Daughter

Two great hemispheres afire,
Staining the sky each moment higher,
Made a double torch of flame
Terrible beyond a name.

Living people ran and fell
Into a huge and fiery well,
Heaving, writhing, till the wind
Like an eye was blotted blind.

Only a hermit here and there
Picked his refuge to the air
And would not let the flame confuse
His wisdom from the way to choose.

One among them, still a child,
Like the oldest hermit smiled.
The hermit's smile was seasoned sure,
Hers was a smile untouched and pure.

And then they saw her turn and pause
For love or pity or some cause,
They saw her watching like a lover
First one fire, then the other.

Was she foolish or at fault?
The only thing that turned to salt
Was something small within her eyes . . . .
Must no one care when a people dies?

News of a Soldier

Life, to me strange, to him was dear.
But he is gone and I am here
And on his earth I move my feet
Which were still when his were fleet.

I see my hand sweat in the sun
As though with labor he has done—
Can I believe now, he submit,
I on the earth, he under it?

At His Funeral

These busy motions have no life at all
Compared to motions death has now unmade;
No living person at his funeral,
Never a moving form of the parade
Affords the power of the silent face,
This gathered energy, ungathering,
Compared to which no passion, no embrace,
No parentage, no pain mean anything.

The Old Men and the Young Men

Said the old men to the young men,
  'Who will take arms to be free?'
Said the young men to the old men,
  'We.'

Said the old men to the young men,
  'It is finished. You may go.'
Said the young men to the old men,
  'No.'

Said the old men to the young men,
  'What is there left to do?'
Said the young men to the old men,
  'You.'

An Old Man Reviews the Wars

Which war is it?
I cannot seem to tell.
There have been so many,
And none has turned out well.

Who fights for whom?
Toward whom are we a foe?
It seems to make no difference,
Now or long ago.

This Flower

These years that cross,
Until you see the loss
Less than the gain,
Are spent in vain.

Landscape and love go blind
With mist to a saddened mind,
Until it remember them
As to this flower the stem.

St. George

Uphold your head with wisdom
And be alert with wrath,
Turn about and find your sword:
There's a monster in your path.

It's a monster immaterial,
Unseen in dark or light,
It's the only monster, dear St. George,
Whom you should ever fight:

Not Satan in his poor disguise
Of scale and forkéd chin,
But your own stiff shadow in the skies
And the shadow far within.

The Fields

Though wisdom underfoot
Dies in the bloody fields,
Slowly the endless root
Gathers again and yields.

In fields where hate has hurled
Its force, where folly rots,
Wisdom shall be uncurled
Small as forget-me-nots.

O Hunted Huntress

O hunted Huntress, up the shore
Springs a white fawn for your dart,
And after you a night-black boar
Closes in upon your heart!
But keep your undeviating eyes
Upon that bright, escaping head—
Aim incessant where he flies,
Follow where those wild feet have fled.
Though you are mortally beset,
Toward the black boar never glance,
Be but swift and so forget
That a bow is no deliverance,
That barbs are slender and would bend
In so uncouth and thick a pelt—
That he would seize you and would rend
The very hand with which you dealt.
Look toward the fawn, the flashing white,
Hope not to flee but to pursue,
Before the onset of the night—
Before the fawn shall blacken too.

Archer

Master, with dart invisible,
Parallel to the dart we see,
How can you pull the fateful string
Of double archery?

How can you pierce an eagle on the wing,
So that the bird will drop and die
And yet its double be transfixed
Forever in the sky?

Winter

Snow

Though he searched the south, the east, the west,
The north too, for a warming breast,
Now in the depth of night he goes
Naked among farthest snows.
For snow, touching the flesh, can warm
As well as fire and do less harm.

Descending Landscape

Snow on the mountain-top,
Blossoms on the lilac-tree,
A white skull on a man.

He has been mountainous,
He has been blossoming,
And shows it if he can.

The Vessel

There lives no beauty, I believed when young,
But at the vessel's prow,
Only the foam is beautiful
Which flies before the voyage and is gone.

There lives no wisdom, I believed when old,
But in the ship's wake
Where the waves
Cover their noise again with the great sea.

The Edge

Long, long before the eyelids harden
And an intake ends the breath,
A body's eyes and a body's burden
Feel the edge of death.

They do not move, they do not think,
They only sit and stare,
The eyes almost ceasing to blink
And the heart ceasing to care.

But it becomes a pleasant thing
To gaze upon the toes
So peacefully dismembering
Before the eyelids close.

Thus Buddha must have sat and known,
Midmost of earth and sea,
The dissolution of the bone
Into its rarity.

No Anodyne

Offer no anodyne
To dreamers who cannot dream alone to their uttermost end.
Befriend
No friend of chance but live unfriended, if ease must be the root
Of friendship. Account no sacrifice divine
But feel the nail
Stand friendly in your foot,
And know that little comes of love but this:
Gethsemane, the soldiers and the kiss
And the pale
Dawn, the perfect loneliness.

Shropshire

Alone he entered through a wood.
Against the moon a gallows stood
And stood alone as he.
And what he had to say he said
And then strode forward and he laid
His cheek against the tree.

None witnessed in that inner wood
How either man or gallows stood
In their nocturnal weather,
But there is much in what he said
Which tells how simply they were wed
Before they lay together.

The Chinese Horseman

There were flutes once merry with stops
And bottles round with wine,
Lips dewy as with attar-drops
And breasts of deep moon-shine—
There were thrushes in the market-rows,
Caught from the circling air,
And no bird sang so true as his,
And there were hills for prayer—
But over the bridge the rider goes,
The rider who was fond,
Leaving what was, crossing what is,
By the bridge that leads beyond—
Beyond the many songs he knew
And sang to lips he kissed,
Beyond the rounded green and blue,
Beyond the mist.

And the scholar who may question him
Will hear only the sound
Of wind-curled waves at the river-brim
And of willows trailing the ground,
And will see the quiet of five bays
Pointing like a hand
Toward the five valleys that divide
The long mountain-land

Beyond the white azalea ways,
Beyond the moonstone wave,
Where no one may be lost nor hide
Nor may be saved nor save,
But where the rider may forego,
And laugh no more nor moan,
And of all pulses never know
Which were his own.

Self

If you were beside me now
  With the setting sun!—
And yet there is room in the evening
  For only one,
And for only one when the dawn
  Is turning white,
And for only one in the day,
  And in the night.

Island

There is an island where a man alone,
Alive beyond the selfishness of living,
Knows the whole world around him as his own
Without resenting and without forgiving.

One's Own Requiem

Oh, now for fewer roofs upon this house,
Only one roof and that a lasting one,
And so for quietude after carouse
And for indifferent feeling of the sun!

Darken me wholly with no lights to close,
Put me to bed beyond a need of sleep,
Let knowledge be the depth a dead man knows
And faith become an easy thing to keep.

Host

His house is wide and deep and tall
And hushed beyond endeavor
Where the most generous host of all
Will let you stay forever.

The Wintry Mind

Winter uncovers distances, I find;
And so the blowing of the wintry mind
Takes leaves away, till there is left behind
A wide cold world. And so the heart grows blind
To the earth's green motions lying warm below
Field upon field, field upon field, of snow.

Adam

There must be, thought Adam, something akin to this
Far mountain I have looked for, a spirit in man
To stay aloft and beautiful and strong,
To change slowly while the body dies
And comes to birth again . . .
I shall beget of my tumult an ocean
To be forever lifted among clouds and returned in rain
To the great ride
Of surf above an infinite tide.

Neighbors

Let me have faith, is what I pray,
    And let my faith be strong,
But who am I, whatever day,
    To know my neighbor wrong?

And though my neighbor may deny
    True faith could be so slight,
May call me wrong, yet who am I
    To know my neighbor right?

We may discover by and by,
    Making our wisdom double,
That he is right and so am I
    And save a lot of trouble.

Gothic

He came home at dusk and at night lay down
   beside his wife, not telling her
About a fold in a dress which was not hers,
   after all. It was a quieter
Fold than any she wore and it had been his handiwork
And he would cut another fold tomorrow,
   alone on his high perch.
He kept feeling that the night made him shirk
Because of darkness and of his staying away from the church
And from his chisel and its cutting and its firm touch
On her robe in that small hidden shadowy place high up
Where people could not see how much
He loved his Virgin. . . . But tomorrow
   was the Seventh Day and Her Son's cup
To think of instead, and no forming
Of the robe, no holy tryst to keep
With Her, no secret fold to shape on Her.
He sighed and felt his wife's breast warming
His mortal heart. And slowly, while he went to sleep,
He dreamed of a garden
In which he was warden,
And of far corners in it where he alone knew
What he had planted and what had faded and what grew.

Grieve Not for Beauty

Grieve not for the invisible, transported brow
On which like leaves the dark hair grew,
Nor for the lips of laughter that are now
Laughing inaudibly in sun and dew,
Nor for those limbs that, fallen low
And seeming faint and slow,
Shall soon
Discover and renew
Their shape and hue—
Like birches varying white before the moon
Or a wild cherry-bough
In spring or the round sea—
And shall pursue
More ways of swiftness than the swallow dips
Among, and find more winds than ever blew
To haven the straining sails of unimpeded ships.

Epithalamium and Elegy

My single constancy is love of life:
Because we have entered no such formal pact
As dulls devotion between man and wife,
No bland acknowledgment, no binding fact,
No mingling of betrothal with divorce,
No dated bliss, no midnight certitude,
No sad necessity, no matter of course,
No pallid answer saying why we wooed;
Because she lets me love her as I can
Moment by moment, moments that always come
Beyond the calculation of a man
For joy or pain, for epithalamium
Or for elegy, and because, when I am spent,
Life shall have had her way, shall be content
Still to confer the sweet bewilderment
On someone else, shall loosen her lovely hair
To the wind, shall turn with bountiful intent
Toward anyone at all, and I not there,
Shall offer cool papayas, pale bamboo
And amorous guava to a later comer,
And none of her gifts, not even a drop of dew,
To me who had received them many a summer.
These are not harlotries but only joy,
These are the very tiptoes of delight.

This is the happiness she gives a boy
With nothing of wickedness, nothing of spite
In that immense, delicious, naked bed
Where anyone may lie, except the dead . . .
But I shall leave her. All that there is of rest
Shall be little enough, after so much of love.
Wherever I move, she is there. Her open breast
Offers the tenderness I am dying of.
Her arm along my body like a snake
Has softly wound me into rings of sleep
And, every time again, stings me awake
And drowns me in her rhythms deep and deep . . .
Can I be tragical, in having had
My love of life by life herself subdued?
Since I am satiate with joy, can I be sad
In leaving? All that there is of solitude
Shall be little enough, after this vast embrace.
Give her some younger lover in my place.

Two Stems

I may be no more split when dead
   Than when I was alive,
For I felt two stems in my earthly bed,
   One seasoned to survive
Filling with the spring's breath,
   The other lost in snow,
And which was life and which was death
   I did not know.

Winter Morning

The hills for miles are stricken into one,
Whiter and simpler than oblivion,
Alive with sudden snow, with sudden sun.

Epilogue

Grasses

Grant me to grasses, fashion me no grief,
Be glad awhile as I was glad before.
For you as well there shall arrive a leaf
Forever swinging better than a door.

A note on the type used in this book

Monotype "Bembo" is the only modern revival of the masterly roman letter cut by Francesco Griffo for Aldus Manutius of Venice in 1495. This face is the prototype from which all "old face" types derive and no later production in that category has ever surpassed the original in dignity and beauty.

Composed by The Stinehour Press, Lunenburg, Vermont. Printed by The Murray Printing Company, Forge Village, Massachusetts. Bound by H. Wolff, New York.

The typography and binding were designed by Roderick D. Stinehour.